STRESS LESS COLORING:
GEOMETRIC PATTERNS

100+ COLORING PAGES FOR PEACE AND RELAXATION

Aadamsmedia

Avon, Massachusetts

Published by
Adams Media, a division of F+W Media, Inc.
57 Littlefield Street, Avon, MA 02322. U.S.A.
www.adamsmedia.com

Contains material adapted from *The Everything® Stress Management Book* by Eve Adamson, copyright ©
2002 by F+W Media, Inc., ISBN 10: 1-58062-578-9, ISBN 13: 978-1-58062-578-4.

ISBN 10: 1-4405-9387-6
ISBN 13: 978-1-4405-9387-1

Printed in the United States of America.

10 9 8 7 6 5 4 3 2 1

Cover design by Sylvia McArdle.
Cover images © iStockphoto.com/egirldesign, Tiax, supermimicry.

This book is available at quantity discounts for bulk purchases.
For information, please call 1-800-289-0963.

INTRODUCTION

Looking to relax? Want to feel more creative? Need more peace and quiet in your life?

If you're looking to get rid of all the extra stress in your life, just pick up a pencil, crayon, or marker and let *Stress Less Coloring: Geometric Patterns* help you manage your worries in a fun, easy, therapeutic way.

Over the years, studies have shown that coloring allows your mind to concentrate solely on the task at hand, which brings you into a restful state similar to what you can achieve through meditation. When you allow yourself to focus on the creative artwork in front of you, your mind doesn't have room for all the anxiety and stress in your life. And when your mind relaxes, your body follows, by letting go of any tension and giving you a sense of peace and well-being.

Throughout the book, you'll find more than 100 black-and-white prints depicting a variety of beautiful geometric patterns that are just waiting to be colored in. And the beauty of these prints is that you can color them in however you'd like. The most relaxing colors are cool shades such as greens, blues, and purples, but if you'd rather splash bold, bright hues like red, yellow, or orange across the page, feel free! Let your own unique palette guide your hand and personalize your pattern.

So whether you're new to art therapy or have been embracing the fun of coloring for years, it's time to stress less and find your inner calm and creativity—one geometric print at a time.

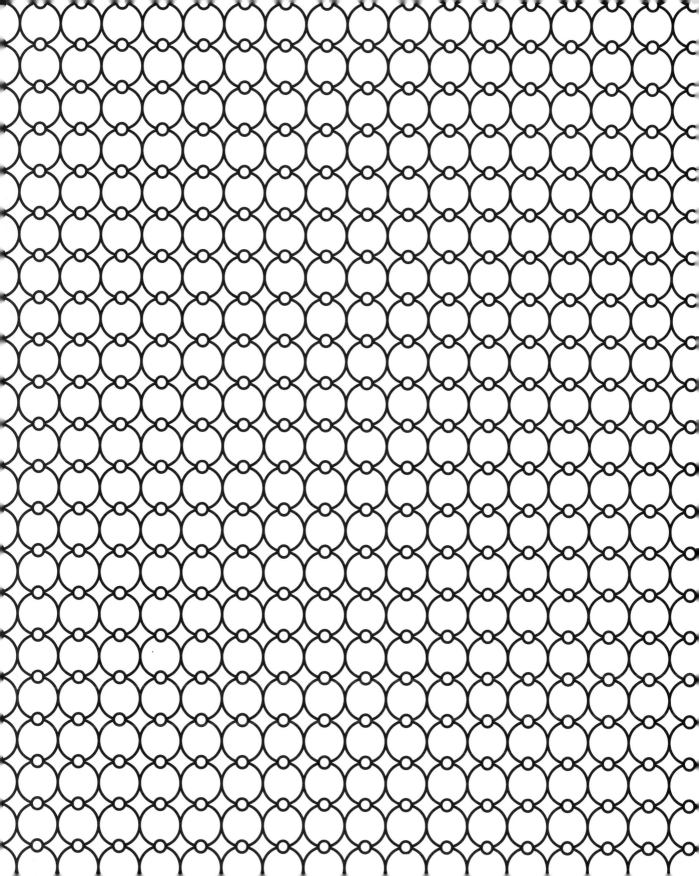

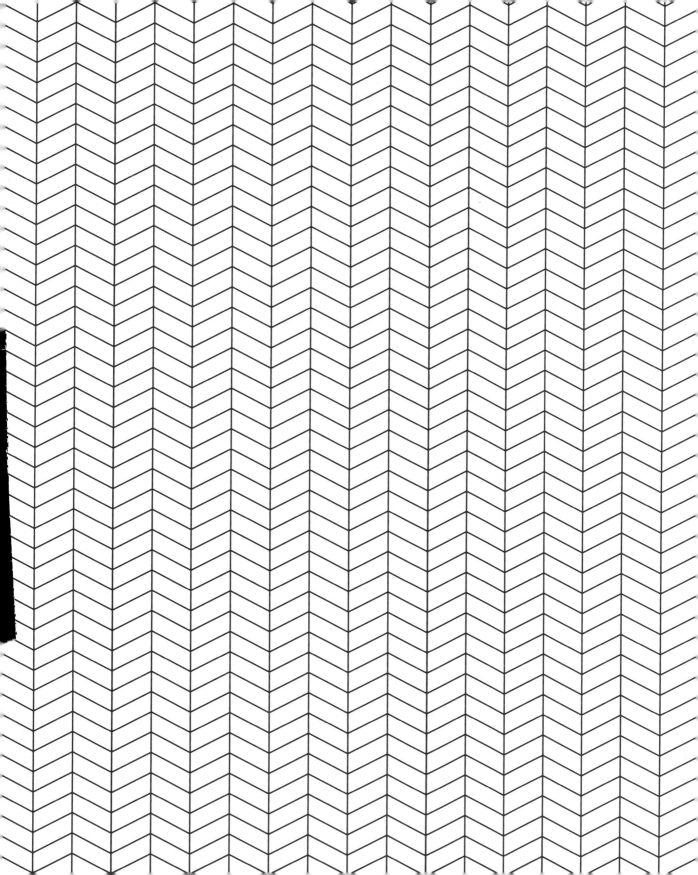

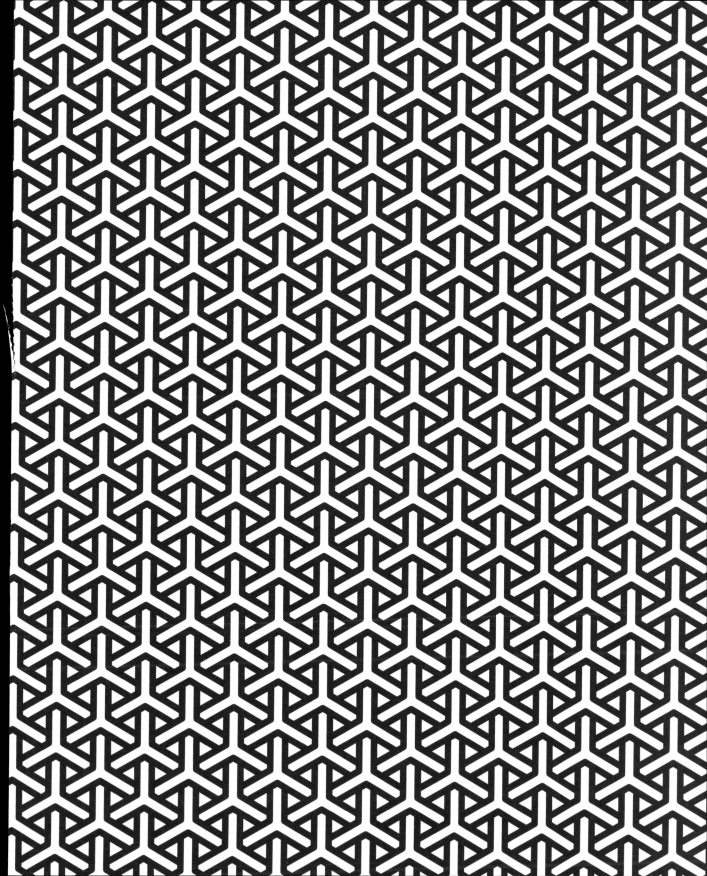

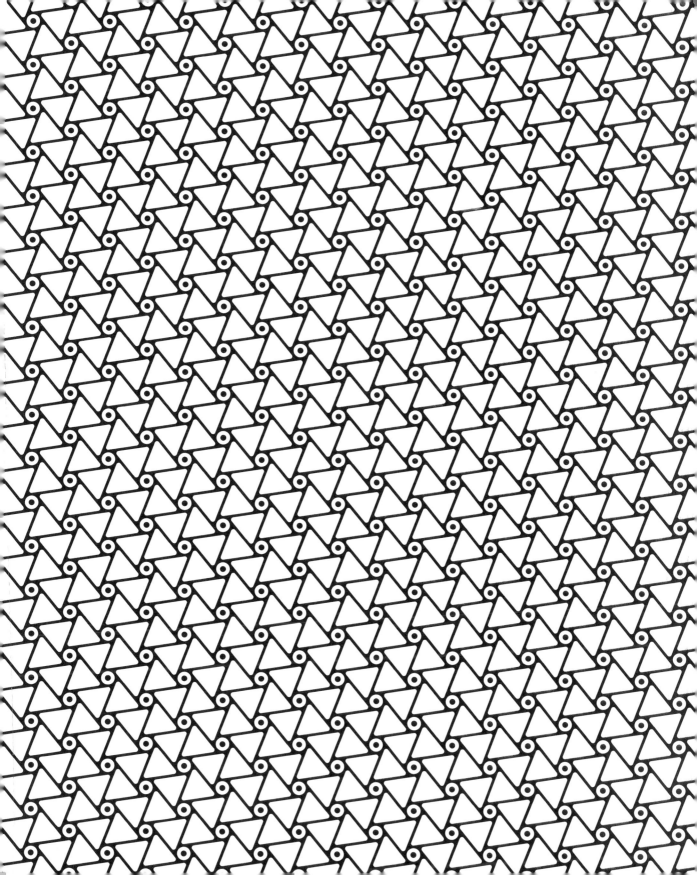

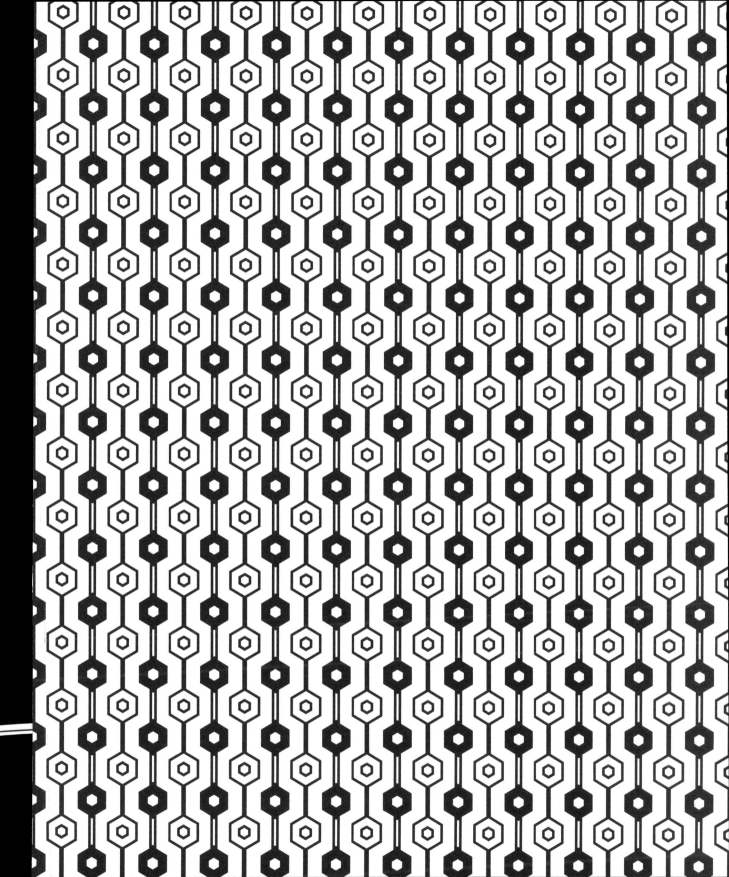

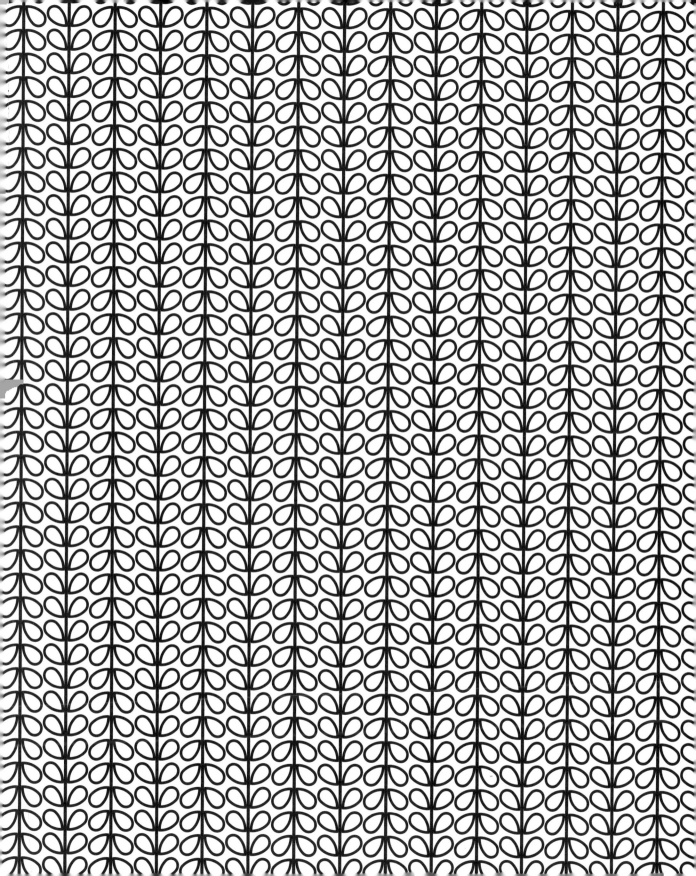

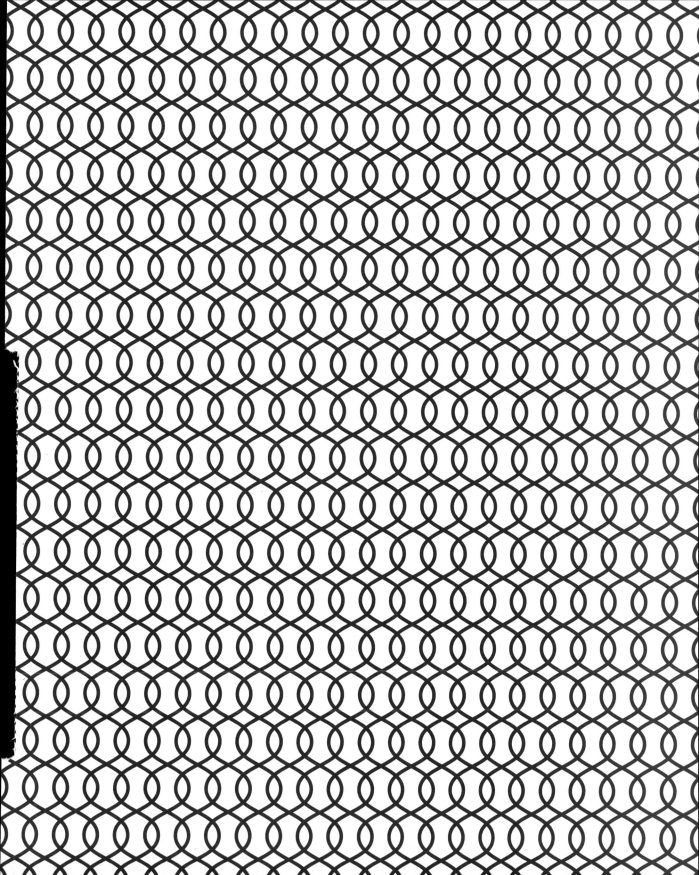

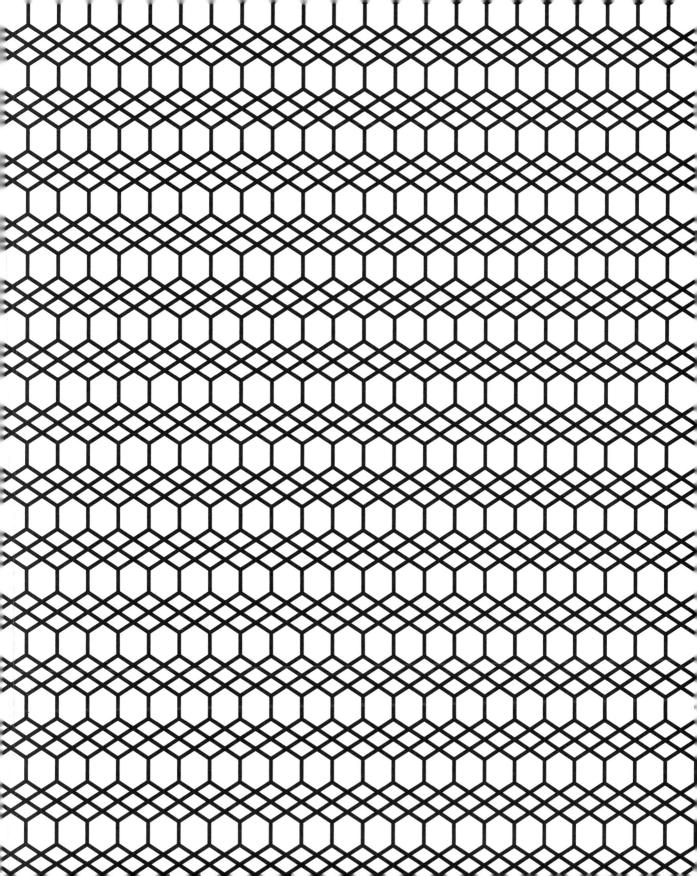

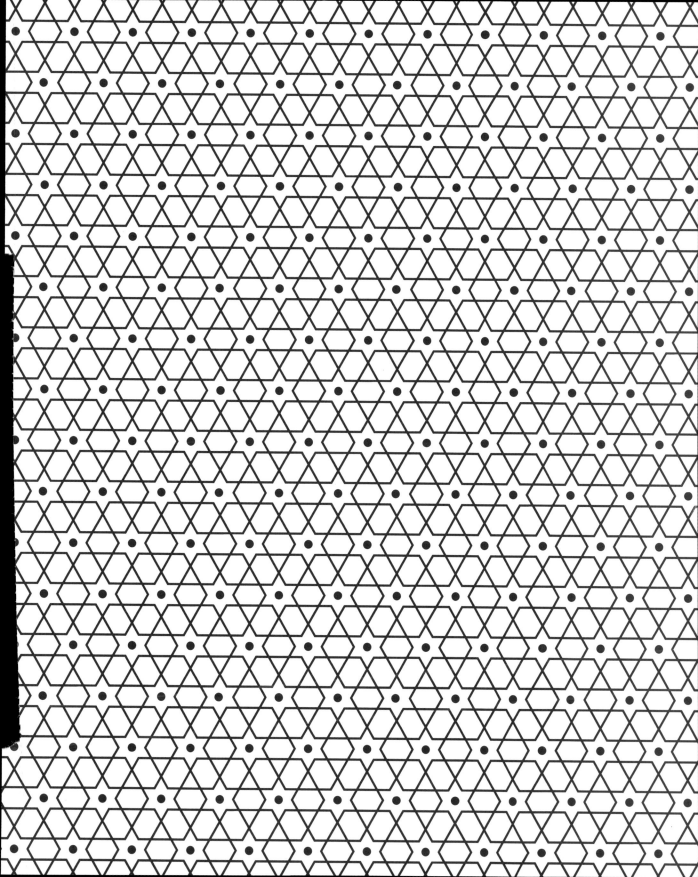

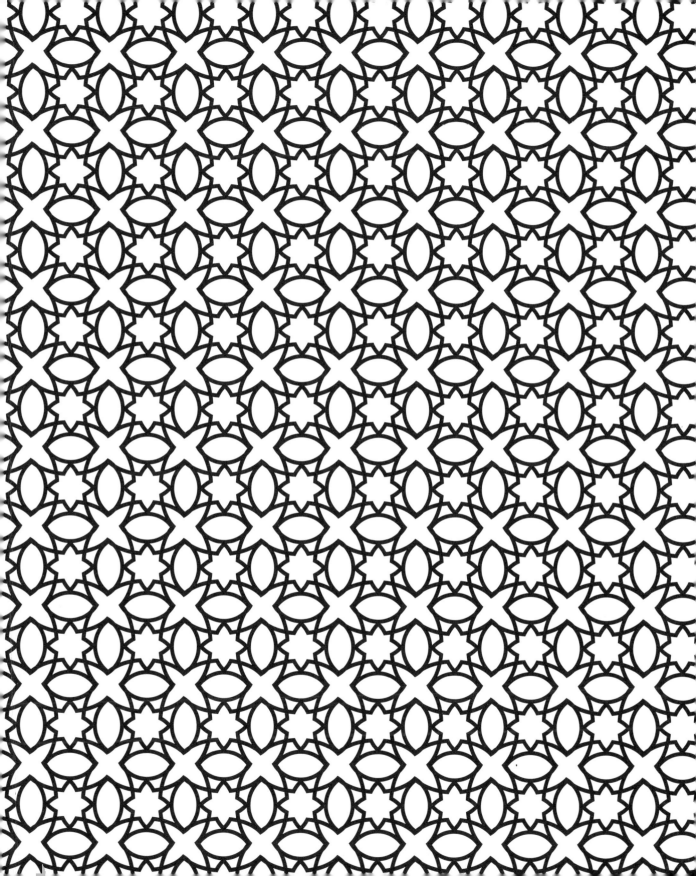

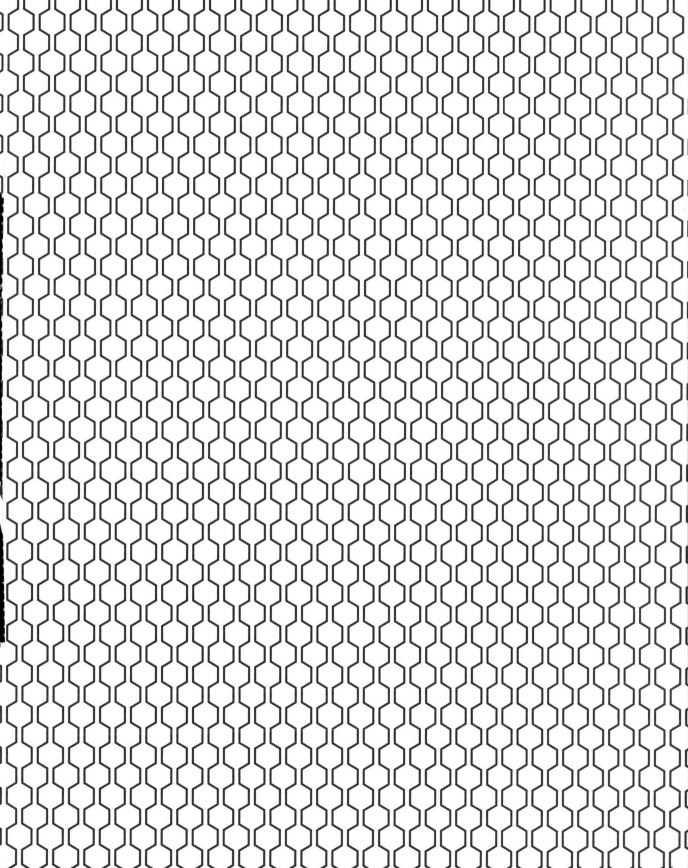

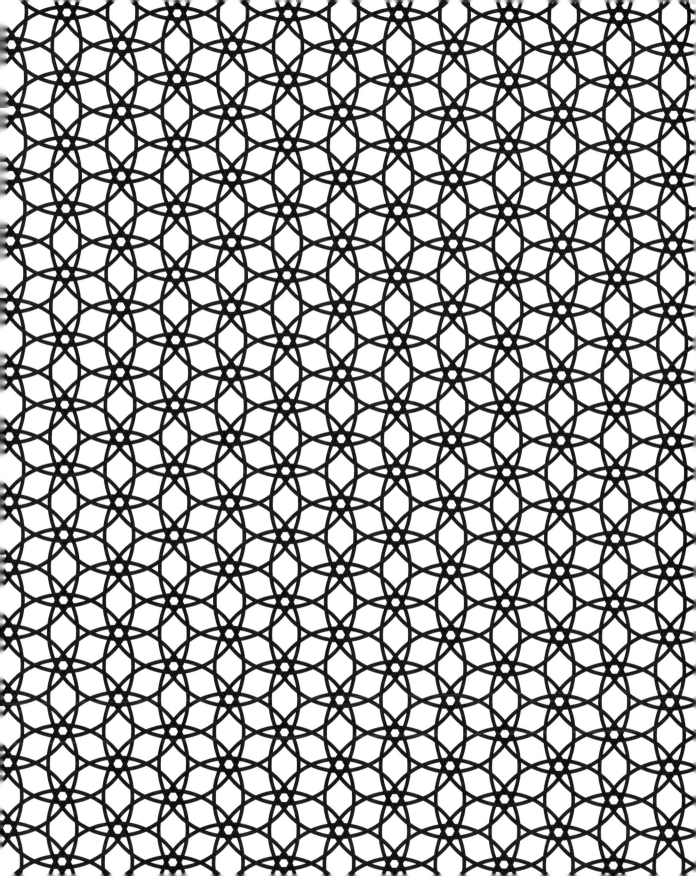